THE GOOD FOOT
At a Glance

The Good Foot at a Glance was written and illustrated by Susan R. Boyd (www.artnanimals.com) and edited by Zachary Franklin, DVM (Templeton and Franklin Veterinary Associates).

The cover picture is a reproduction of a painting by Siobhan Nicholls, an artist, ACEHP Australian Certified Equine Hoofcare Practitioner, and friend. (http://dreamingofdarkhorses.art/)

Dedicated to the memory of
Dreamer and to every person
who has ever rescued an
abandoned or abused horse

A portion of the profits from
this booklet will be donated
to animal rescue groups

Disclaimer

Please understand that just as each horse is unique, so are their hooves. The differences might be attributed to circumstances of the horse's genes, breed, environment, diet, activity or a condition from birth.

For this reason, the hoof should never be trimmed or carved to try to meet any standards of hoof model or conformation.

The descriptions in this booklet are for the horse owner who does not have the knowledge or experience to have developed an "eye" for healthy hoof conformation. The guidelines define a static view of a healthy hoof (front and side views while standing and bottom or solar view when lifted). The most important "view" however is the dynamic view (from impact to breakover) during stride when the hoof is loaded (weight bearing) and unloaded and it flexes and distorts as a result of movement and ground pressure. Shock, pressure and release, are the stimulus for growth, both normal and abnormal. The condition and shape of each of the structures that make up the part of hoof you can see, plus the shock and pressure applied during stride influence the condition, shape, growth, and function of the internal structures you cannot see. Each part of the hoof, those you can see and those inside, all depend on each other to function properly. When one part is off balance with the others, inappropriate growth may result and could affect the function and health of the entire foot (and possibly the entire horse. No hoof – No horse). The correct dimensional balance (medial/lateral = side to side, dorsal/palmar = front to back, distal/proximal = top to bottom, and yaw = around) of the hoof and each of its individual parts is critical to allow for appropriate stimulus for healthy growth of the entire hoof inside and out. You can build hoof soundness but can never carve it into a hoof.

The hoof can only be as strong as the terrain it lives on. Horses that live on shavings in a stall and/or on grass pasture will not have hooves as strong as those that live on a varied terrain that includes gravel and rock and will not be able to travel comfortably on gravel or rock without protection.

I am not a professional hoof care specialist. I am a horse owner. I trim my own horses' feet as best I can. This is not meant to be a trimming guide or replace veterinarian or hoof care professional advice. For specific details related to your horse and his hoof care, what might be normal or abnormal for his specific conformation, refer to your hoof care professional and/or your veterinarian.

THE GOOD FOOT
At a Glance

*A horse owner's guide to
the visual aspects of
a healthy hoof*

Susan R Boyd

THE GOOD FOOT AT A GLANCE
Table of Contents

Written and illustrated by Susan R Boyd
Edited by Zachary Franklin, DVM

ABOUT THE AUTHORS

Susan R Boyd and Ice

As early as I can remember, I wanted a horse. I bought my first horse in my mid-twenties when I was married. My horse was kept at a boarding facility where he was fed and cared for by the owners of the facility. I loved my horse but I knew nothing about how to care for him. I moved out of state and left my horse with my parents some 40 years ago. About 10 years ago I decided to adopt a horse which would be kept on my property. My lack of knowledge and inexperience made it impossible for me to properly care for my horse or to know if the people I depended on were doing a good job.

I depend a great deal on instinct. It has served me well throughout my life and I found that I had some strong instincts about caring for my horse. A combination of instincts, education and experience form the foundation

2

for the care I give my horses now. My instincts tell me that I want my horses to live as close as possible to a natural life style (based on the way they evolved in nature). In my search to learn how to care for my seven horses (all rescues except one), I have taken the following clinics/courses:

Natural Horsemanship Clinic - Ginger Krenz

Barefoot Trimming Clinic - Cheryl Henderson

Applied Equine Podiatry – K. C. LaPierre

NRC Plus (Equine Nutrition) – Dr. Eleanor Kellon

Nutrition as Therapy – Dr. Eleanor Kellon

Insulin Resistance/Cushing's – Dr. Eleanor Kellon

Deworming Horses – Dr. Eleanor Kellon

Horse Care – University of Florida

Equine Nutrition – University of Edinburgh

Technical Large Animal Emergency Rescue – Dr. Rebecca Gimenez

Hoof Rehabilitation Workshop – Pete Ramey

Horsemanship Principles – Carson James

Riding Lessons – Ann Marie Morgan, Miami Int'l Riding Club

I currently live in South Florida with my barefoot horses and several other critters. I want the best for my horses and believe that the more I know, the better my best will be. I do my best to keep things as natural as possible.

Zachary Franklin, DVM and Drako

Dr. Zachary Franklin has been my equine veterinarian from the beginning of my adventure into horse ownership. He has helped me care for my horses and supported me in my educational journey to do my best to keep things healthy and natural for my horses. Dr. Franklin is a contributor to this booklet and he graciously edited every page to insure quality, accuracy of content, and presentation. Dr. Franklin is a graduate of Ohio State University and has been practicing in the Miami area, Templeton and Franklin Veterinary Associates, since 1993.

INTRODUCTION

If you look up "horse hoof" in Wikipedia, it describes the hoof as:

> A **horse hoof** is a structure surrounding the distal phalanx of the 3rd digit (digit III of the basic pentadactyl limb of vertebrates, evolved into a single weight-bearing digit in equids) of each of the four limbs of Equus species, which is covered by complex soft tissue and keratinized (cornified) structures. Since a single digit must bear the full proportion of the animal's weight that is borne by that limb, the hoof is of vital importance to the horse. The phrase "no hoof, no horse" underlines how much the health and the strength of the hoof is crucial for horse soundness.

The domestication of horses has solved some horse care problems for owners but has created many problems for the horse:

- In the wild horses travel 15 or more miles a day over a variety of terrains which is required for overall health and exercise plus proper exfoliation and growth of the hoof. Many Domestic horses stand alone in stalls or small paddocks.

- Wild horses live and travel in a herd which allows interaction and safety. Many domestic horses are housed alone.

- As trickle feeders, horses eat small amounts of low nutritional forage all day long in the wild which is required to protect their digestive system and maintain health. The domestic horse gets 2 or 3 meals a day of hay plus a processed feed/grain or rich pasture that usually contain lots of sugar and starch.

- Horses that live in the wild adapt to changing weather conditions and thermoregulate their body temperature accordingly. The domestic horse is clipped or shaved and sometimes blanketed. They look great but can no longer regulate their own body temperature or use facial hairs to protect vulnerable areas of the face and head.

All of these changes to their natural life style affect the overall health (both physical and emotional) of the horse and consequently the health of their feet. It is our responsibility as horse owners to do the best we can in domestic conditions to give proper care to our horses. This booklet only addresses one small piece of the horse, the external (visual) hoof, and only gives the horse owner a model to start with. A healthy hoof is the result of good nutrition, proper living conditions/environment, the right exercise, and a proper hoof trim.

The information in this booklet is a result of research I gathered from the experts in the field of hoof care (farriers, hoof care practitioners, veterinarians, equine nutritionists, blacksmiths, universities specializing in horse care). I compiled data regardless of professional source, breed, or discipline, barefoot or shod and put it together in this booklet. The information is not my opinion but is a combination of current opinion/science of the experts. This booklet is meant to be a general guideline that will give the non-professional horse owner a visual base (external anatomical picture of the equine hoof- what you see) to help them recognize a good hoof or a potential problem. I do not address hoof problems or treatments at all. Many horse owners are under the misconception that if a horse is not lame, it has healthy feet. As with people if we do not recognize what is healthy, (heart function, blood pressure, blood sugar, bone density, cholesterol, etc.), we may not realize we have a health problem until it becomes critical (heart attack, stroke, weak broken bones, clogged arteries, diabetes etc.).

> *Dr. Debra Taylor, DVM, MS, DACVIM-LA, Associate Professor, Department of Clinical Sciences College of Veterinary Medicine, Auburn University. "We see so much pathology that we would not recognize a healthy foot if we saw it".*

Use this booklet as a tool, a guideline to ask questions of your hoof care professional or veterinarian but please keep in mind, you (the owner) are responsible for the diet, environment, exercise, type of trim (and the application of instructions from your hoof care specialist and/or veterinarian) that will keep your horse healthy and standing and moving on sound healthy feet. So, do the best you can by learning.

HOOF – SOLAR VIEW

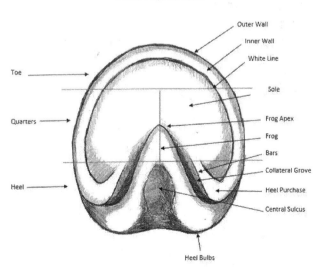

CHAPTER 1:
THE HOOF CAPSULE

Definition of the hoof capsule: For the purpose of this booklet it is the outer element of the hoof made of hard keratinized horn which functions as a "wrapper" protecting the inner structures of the hoof.

A good healthy hoof capsule should have no cracking or chipping nor should there be any growth or stress rings. The capsule should be symmetrical and not concave or convex. As a general rule, the front hoof is round and symmetrical, and the hind is a bit more oval and generally asymmetrical.

Front Foot   Hind Foot

The hoof is divided into four parts or quarters (toe, heel, inside or medial quarter and outside or lateral quarter). The walls on the sides (medial and lateral quarters) should be of equal height sloping slightly outward from top (coronet) to bottom (ground) with the medial quarter (inside) often being a little steeper (more upright) than the lateral quarter (outside). The coronet should be even without bulges or dips. The circumference of the hoof wall should be medially and laterally symmetric. New hoof wall growth from the coronet should have consistent downward angulation. On the barefoot horse there is a slight arch on the medial and lateral quarters at the ground to allow for flexion/distortion. This arch is natural on a feral horse and trimmed on a domestic barefoot horse if not present naturally.

Coronet

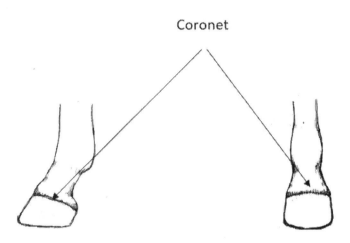

Some hoof care practitioners look for angles when viewing the hoof. There is considerable variation in what might be considered as normal hoof angulation, how it is measured, or in some cases if it is even important. It was necessary for me to use angles in order to provide a picture of what a healthy foot should look like. The following angle measurements are generally considered acceptable as a model regardless of breed or discipline.

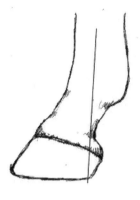

Ideally, when viewed from the side, an imaginary line should bisect the lower leg and intersect the back of the hoof at the ground.

An imaginary straight line that bisects the fetlock joint should intersect at the coronet with an imaginary straight line that runs to the ground. Note the toe and heel angles are parallel to each other and to the straight line.

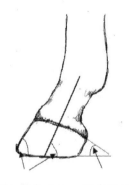

45 to 50 degrees   30 degrees

The imaginary lines form angles. The toe angle should closely approximate the heel forming a 45 to 50 degree angle to the ground on the front hoof and 50 to 55 on the hind. If visible, the tubules (colored vertical lines running from coronet to ground) should parallel the toe and heel angles. The coronet should be straight and form about a 30 degree angle to the ground at the heel

11

In general, the front feet are less steep than the hind feet and the heel angle will vary according to the individual toe angles which should be in a straight line of growth from the coronet to the toe at the center.

Again, I stress that this information should only be used as a guideline to give you an idea of what a healthy hoof should look like. Horses are unique and if you see differences between this information and what you see on your horse, you should discuss it with your hoof care professional or veterinarian.

Chapter 2:
Heel Purchase

Definition of Heel Purchase (also known as the angle of the bar, angle of the wall, or heel buttress): These terms are all used to describe the rearmost point of the hoof wall. On a solar view (looking at the hoof from the bottom) it is the point at which both side walls turn abruptly inward toward the toe forming the bars.

The most palmar (rearmost) aspect of the heel purchase should be nearly parallel to or slightly forward of the widest part of the frog. At impact, during stride when the heel strikes the ground, the heel purchase takes the greatest amount of force so a good amount of surface or purchase area is desirable and proper location insures that the ground reactive forces are dealt with correctly.

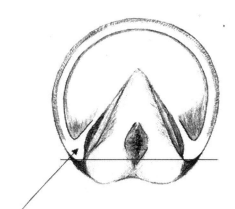

Heel Purchase   Parallel to widest part of the frog

CHAPTER 3:
BARS

Definition of Bars: The bars are an extension of the hoof wall. They extend beyond the heel purchase bordering the outside of the collateral grooves on the solar aspect (bottom) of the foot ending about mid-frog.

Bars should stand fairly erect, not folded over, and should be straight on the dorsal to palmar plane (front to back) having a slight outward angle opposing that of the frog. In a properly functioning foot, the outer wall of the bars will be worn, or broken away at sole level. A properly structured bar runs from the heel purchase and follows the concavity of the live sole along the side of the frog, until blending into the sole about half way down the frog.

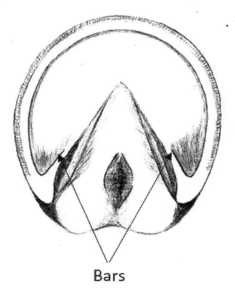

Bars

CHAPTER 4:
FROG

Definition of frog: The frog is a wedge shaped mass, a triangular pad of soft elastic horn which makes up the back two thirds of the foot and occupies the area between the bars at the back of the sole. The **central sulcus** is the inner crease of the frog located centrally in the back half of the frog about the size of a tangerine segment.

The frog should be centered in the foot. The frog and heel bulbs are one seamless unit. A wide substantial frog is considered more suitable. When the foot is functioning properly, the frog will shed or be exfoliated evenly. The width of the frog should be at least 50 to 67% of the length of the frog. The height should reach the bearing surface (touch the ground) but not exceed ¼ inch above the live sole at the widest part of the foot. The central sulcus should be wide and shallow with no evidence of infection. A deep central sulcus is unhealthy and is evidence of a weak frog and possibly thrush. To function properly the frog should be healthy, full and firm to the touch (not full of holes and cracks), and free of thrush. The frog is one of the most important structures of the foot. A healthy frog provides the stimulus for healthy growth of the collateral cartilages, digital cushion, bars, and heel purchase and aids with blood circulation within the hoof.

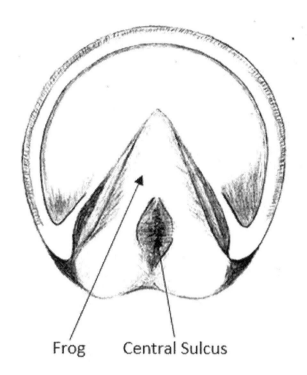

Frog   Central Sulcus

CHAPTER 5:
COLLATERAL GROOVES

Definition of Collateral Grooves (also known as Collateral Sulci, lateral and medial grooves): The collateral grooves are grooves that are located adjacent to and running parallel to the frog (The seam or crease between the frog and the bars).

The collateral grooves between the frog and the bars follow the concavity of the sole and are usually deeper at the back of the hoof sloping upward toward the apex of the frog. They are sometimes used to estimate sole thickness and distance between coffin bone and ground. In a healthy, fully functional hoof the average depth at the apex of the frog would be about 10 to 20mm off the ground (not including wall height). The distance off the ground at the back, adjacent to the bars at their deepest point, would be about 15 to 30mm. Very deep collateral grooves can be an indication of excessive false sole. Very shallow collateral grooves can be an indication of thin sole. It is important to clean the collateral grooves when picking out the hoof. They tend to trap dirt, manure, and stones and are often the starting point for thrush and canker.

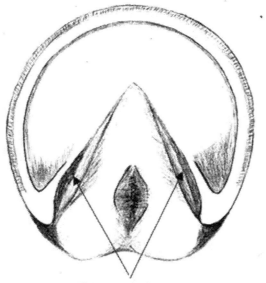

Collateral Grooves

CHAPTER 6:
SOLE

Definition of Sole: The sole is the bottom portion of hoof that lies between the wall, bars, and frog. Live sole looks similar to ivory and receives nutrition from the corium below. **Retained sole or false sole** is sole that is no longer receiving nutrition and under normal conditions will exfoliate. Retained sole usually appears dry and cracked and often chalky

Live sole provides resistance, support, protection, and stimulus for proper growth to the inner structures of the hoof. The sole should be balanced medially – laterally (side to side). Sole thickness varies from horse to horse. Proper thickness of sole is crucial to maintaining soundness in the horse. A sole with proper structure should exfoliate evenly throughout, leaving a slight concavity to front feet and somewhat greater concavity in the rear feet. A thick calloused live sole with concavity is considered to be healthy and functional. The sole will adapt to terrain conditions and a horse that lives on hard flat terrain will have less concavity than those that live on soft or uneven terrain. Both should have adequate collateral groove depth. A healthy sole should be firm to the touch. Live sole resembles ivory or soapstone and should never be removed during a trim. A thin layer of exfoliating sole is thought by some to be protective, especially on thin soled horses where natural exfoliation is preferable. On the barefoot horse (the natural hoof) the outer perimeter of the sole is load bearing along with the inner hoof wall. On shod horses the load distribution, usually on the outer wall, will vary according to the trim, type of shoe, placement and use of padding materials).

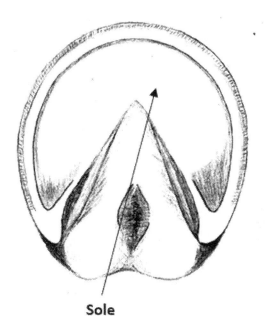

Sole

CHAPTER 7:
WHITE LINE

Definition of White Line (also called the golden line): The white line is the yellow or golden area located between the junction of the sole and the inner wall. The white line runs vertically between the inner wall and the laminae* from the area just below the coffin bone to the ground. The white line isolates the sensitive structures of the internal foot from infiltration of foreign bodies.

   In the properly functioning foot, the white line should appear tight with no bruising. A small amount of material is often abraded away at ground level creating a shallow crease around the circumference of the hoof. This crease often fills with dirt helping to provide increased traction. A tight healthy white line effectively prevents infiltration of bacteria that may otherwise cause the abscess known as gravel (seedy toe or white line disease).

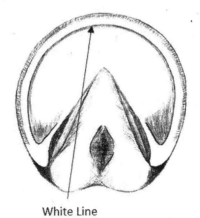

White Line

*Note: This booklet is about the parts of the hoof that you can see. Although you can only see the area where the white line ends at the bottom of the hoof, because a healthy white line is critical to a good foot, a more detailed description is provided here:

In a healthy situation, in the upper 4/ 5 or so of the hoof capsule, the epidermal laminae (which are literally a part of the hoof wall) are bonded with the dermal laminae (which are firmly connected to the coffin bone). After the wall growth grows past the coffin bone (thus past the dermal laminae and the corium) the epidermal laminae continue to the ground along with the rest of the hoof wall. From that point down the epidermal laminae become bonded with the sole. The white line is the hoof wall's bond with the sole. It is made up of 50% epidermal laminae and 50% sole.

CHAPTER 8:
HOOF WALL

Definition of Hoof Wall: The hoof wall is the outer protective structure of the foot. It consists of three main layers:

- **Periople**, just below the coronet. Its main function is to bridge the junction between the skin and the hoof wall keeping out dirt and infection and provides protection for new outer wall growth. This layer disintegrates as it moves down the hoof.
- **Outer wall**, composed of pigmented horn which forms a hard protective barrier that prevents the loss or addition of moisture between the wall and inner structures of the hoof.
- **Inner wall**, is non-pigmented, less hard and a little more flexible than the outer wall and acts as a buffer between the harder outer wall and the more delicate structures of the inner foot.

A good healthy hoof wall will have an outer wall (pigmented area) with no growth rings, chipping, or cracking and an inner wall (non-pigmented area) with an even thickness from toe to heel and a good strong connection between the two. The hoof wall can be dark in color, almost white, or a combination. Although some believe lighter colored hooves are weaker, there is no scientific proof of this.

The bottom of the hoof wall is trimmed to a flat surface to accommodate a shoe. On the shod foot the outer and inner walls are load bearing. On the barefoot horse the outer wall is trimmed (rolled or beveled, referred to as a mustang roll) so the inner wall and outer perimeter of the sole are load bearing and the outer wall bears little to no weight. It is commonly believed that it takes an average of 12 months for the hoof wall to grow from hairline (coronet) to the ground.

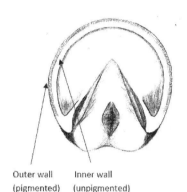

Outer wall   Inner wall
(pigmented)   (unpigmented)

Periople

CHAPTER 9:
HEEL BULBS

Definition of Heel Bulbs: The area of the heel at the back of the hoof covered in soft tissue of periople, skin and hide that merges with the frog as one seamless unit.

There is a medial and a lateral heel bulb (inside and outside). Healthy heel bulbs should be equal in size and height. They should feel firm to the touch and be free of cracks and holes, and thrush and abscess free. Healthy heel bulbs will have some distance between them and not be pushed toward the center as to form a crease between the two which is an indication of contracted heels. Heel bulbs which differ in height are known as sheared heels and are a sign of uneven weight loading.

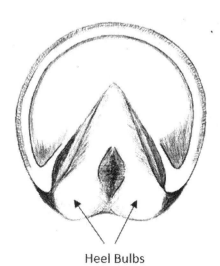

Heel Bulbs

27

CHAPTER 10:
LATERAL CARTILAGE AND DIGITAL CUSHION

Definition of Lateral Cartilage (also known as collateral cartilage or ungular cartilage): The lateral cartilage of the hoof is attached to the palmar/plantar (rear/lower) processes of the coffin bone on both the lateral and medial (outside and inside) sides. It wraps around each side to the dorsal (top/front) area of the hoof just under the coronet. The lateral cartilage plays a major role in storing and releasing energy during stride.

Definition of Digital Cushion (also known as plantar cushion): The digital cushion is an elastic structure which is wedge shaped and occupies the lower rear area of the hoof. It is bordered by the lateral cartilages at the sides and by the frog below. The base lies under the skin at the back of the hoof and is divided by a depression into two rounded masses forming part of the heel bulbs. It plays a major part in reducing concussion to both the coffin and navicular bones; and on the hoofs ability to expand, flex and distort on impact.

The lateral cartilages and digital cushion form the foundation for (and support) the back half of the hoof (the coffin bone is the foundation for the front of the hoof).

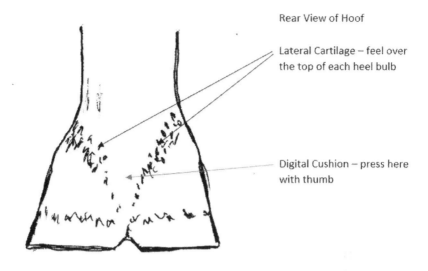

Rear View of Hoof

Lateral Cartilage – feel over the top of each heel bulb

Digital Cushion – press here with thumb

Although the lateral cartilages and digital cushion are not visible, I have included them in this booklet <u>because they are critically important structures and although not visible, you can feel them</u>. The lateral cartilages and digital cushion are the soft tissues that make up the back half of the hoof. One cannot stress enough the importance of the health of these two structures relative to the health of the entire hoof. In a healthy hoof the digital cushion will feel firm and just a little yielding when pressed with the thumb. It should not feel soft and mushy. When healthy the lateral cartilages will feel firm, flexible and lay over the top of the heel bulb. An unhealthy lateral cartilage will feel more upright. In the illustration below I point out where you can feel the structures.

THE BAREFOOT HORSE – A LIFESTYLE

"The barefoot horse" is not just a description of a horse without shoes nor is it just a description of the hoof condition of a horse. Rather, it is a description of a lifestyle of a horse.

The lifestyle of a barefoot horse includes:

- A free choice, forage based diet which is low in sugar, low in starch, and balanced to have the correct amount and ratios of vitamins and minerals for the type of hay being fed.
- Living conditions and environment which allow for and encourage movement over several different types of terrain including grass, gravel, and rock.
- Daily exercise that includes walking, trotting and cantering. Horses in open range situations will travel 15 or more miles a day.
- A proper barefoot trim every 4 to 6 weeks. Some horses can go longer if the environment promotes some self-trimming.

A healthy bare foot either develops from birth or is encouraged to develop later in adult life when the horse owner decides the barefoot lifestyle is what they desire for their horse. All the conditions listed above play an important role in developing and maintaining a healthy horse with healthy feet. It is not just a matter of removing the horse shoes. When a person decides to become a marathon runner, they need to train. They need to eat right, give up the couch potato lifestyle, and exercise to condition muscles, bone, lungs, legs and feet. The entire body must be conditioned and wearing the correct foot protection is critical. They have to start slow and work gradually to condition their entire body. It is no different with a horse transitioning to a barefoot lifestyle.

REFERENCES:

Care and Rehabilitation of the Equine Foot – Pete Ramey

Making Natural Hoof Care Work For You – Pete Ramey

The Lame Horse – James R. Rooney

Feed Your Horse Like A Horse – Juliet M. Getty

Hickman's Farriery – John Hickman & Martin Humphrey

The Chosen Road – K.C. LaPierre

Horse Journal – Eleanor Kellon

The Natural Horse – Jaime Jackson

Horse Owners GuideTo Natural Hoof Care – Jaime Jackson

Paddock Paradise – Jaime Jackson

Notes

Notes

Made in the USA
San Bernardino, CA
09 June 2018